Altars of Ordinary Li

June Sylvester Saraceno

Plain View Press
P. O. 42255
Austin, TX 78704

plainviewpress.net
sb@plainviewpress.net
1-512-441-2452

Cover photo by Ed Book (edbookphoto.com), a freelance
photographer, who was following Mother Nature across Wyoming
when this image found him.

Acknowledgments

My thanks to the editors of the journals in which the following
poems were previously published. "Wings," *Ash Canyon Review*,
2005; "The Wall," *California Quarterly*, 2007; "Still Life with
Apples," *California Quarterly*, 1992; "Blue Trajectory," "The
Accident Inside" and "Late February," *Ginosko*, 2007; "She
Said," *Maverick Press* 1996; "Tracks," *Moonshine Ink*, 2003;
"Chrysanthemums and the Communist Manifesto," The Pedestal,
2004; "The Calling," The Rebel, 1980; "Finding My Way Back,"
Silk Road, 2007; "She Waves Goodbye from the Window," *Smartish
Pace*, 2000, reprinted by permission in *Sunspinner* 2006; "In Avon,"
Tar River Poetry, 1991.

Thanks to Wendy Maltz, editor of the anthologies *Passionate
Hearts* in which "Palms" was first published, and *Intimate Kisses* in
which "The Ordinary Day" first appeared.

The following poems, or earlier versions of them, also appeared in
my chapbook *Mean Girl Trips* published by Pudding House Press,
fall 2006: "Remembering Tinky's," "Carson City Drum Circle,"
"Bar in Bavaria," "August Air of D.C.," "Au Pair," "Seagulls of
Vancouver," "Mannequins," "Altars/City Lights," and "Elevator."

Contents

Three   67

for my loves, Anthony and Dylan

With Gratitude

Special thanks to the following people for love, light and laughter along the way: Robin Griffin for lifelong love, support and encouragement; Marisella Veiga for laughing, crying, editing and always being in my corner; Peter Makuck, my mentor and beloved poetry professor; Allison Hilborn for not giving up and not letting me give up; Suzanne Roberts for valuable editing ideas.

A special thanks as well to my family and family of friends for their faith and encouragement over the years: Linda, David, Julia, Lewis, Kat, Amy, Anne, Pam, Kim, Colleen, Leslie, LeeAnn, Madonna, Grace, Deirdre, Louise, Mitch, Lori, Jane, Mary, Joanne, Nicole, Sylvia, Melanie, Donna, Tom, Nancy and all the rest, you know who you are.

I am deeply grateful to Susan Bright, my editor and publisher, for her incisive editing, her commitment to publishing this book, and her generous support of my work.

One

In Avon

for my mother Mary Gray Sylvester (1928-1984)

My mother was part of the landscape,
her eyes bluer than sound or ocean,
her sandy hands catching us up.
One day in 1969 she sat
on a bleached out piece of driftwood
long enough for a photograph
to catch her between sky and sea.

In the village the oval ESSO sign creaked
above the abandoned service station.
The village idiot walked the streets
muttering under his breath
in some strange tongue.
We would follow giggling, at a distance,
all the way to Gray's general store,
dimly lit and full of poor-boy-cakes,
fireballs, sweet tarts.
On the way back
past the harbor, rank with the smell of fish
past the church, with its ominous bell
past the brambly blackberry bushes,
we'd come to her home,
the big house with the banisters
the iron beds, cement cistern
and fig trees,
a curious Eden,
the primary ground of her existence.

In Avon my mother walked
barefoot through her girlhood.
Years later we followed her paths,
dug in the clam beds,

Continued

caught the lightening bugs,
sneaked out after dark to count stars
or spy on adults
sitting around the kitchen table
with their mugs of coffee and conversation.

Each summer we returned,
as if by instinct, to Avon
where the frogs filled the air at night
with a terrible noise,
shiny green they'd climb the screens
and cling there.
My mother floated moon-like
in our doorway.
She'd remind us to say our prayers
before she said good night.

The Calling

I have learned to recognize the warm
vaguely oniony smell of my mother's hands,
the essence of her calling.

At twelve, I was going to be an artist.
I drew my mother bent over the oven
sweat damp hair clinging to her neck.

On Sundays, I sat stiff on hard benches.
I listened to the stories. Mary sat
at Jesus' feet, but Martha was busy in her kitchen.

I wander out in the evening,
Mother calls from the kitchen window.
Her face is framed, crossed and hung in the panes.

The years made Mother smaller.
She looks at me and shakes her head.
She says *settle down…good Christian man…family.*

My lovers say I'm distant, or insecure.
I nod my head, watch their jawline move
see how hard they swallow.

Sometimes I raise my music up,
I send my voice out.
I split my own silence with song.

Mother says *don't be loud…turn it down a notch*
your father is sleeping
come help with supper if you will…

I will, I will (not my will but thine).

Continued

Mother says I'm headed down the wrong path.
She shakes her head, while the stove that heats her heaven
consumes
and consumes.

Making Peace

for my father Dwight Sylvester 1928-2002

The angry years spun by,
the distance grew loud between us
until your disease left you stricken into silence,
immobile on the improvised hospital bed
in your living room.
I returned as your life waned.
Between us, I was the sole voice.
This reversal, an empty irony,
leaves me mute and staring
at your gray face on the pillow.

Your old black bible between us on the nightstand
offers its own weight of words.
Familiar and heavy, I lift it
knowing any bitter taunt you might have made
will stay dried on your tongue, unvoiced.

I silently call a truce and leaf through the thin onion skin pages
searching for Psalms to slake your thirst.
You've highlighted every page yellow.
I glance over the passages randomly and begin to read
about old battles, wrathful words, a plea
to God to smite the enemy.
These are not the words I have searched for.

I remember Psalm 23 and turn the pages back,
speak these words,
until I can hear myself reciting at the dinner table,
a thin sing-song of memorization,
an echo of the child you once had.

Continued

What is left unsaid between us
will remain unsaid.
The heart has its own language
and blood will tell its story.

But for now, the wheel has turned
in the shadow of your death.
Even old enemies can lie down
in green pastures
and fear no evil.

Finding My Way Back

When I was a child, fairy tales gave me hives.
Hansel and Gretel must have known
bread crumbs could never lead them home,
casseroles for the dead are crusted over with them.
Better to save those crumbs for starving days
than try to unravel a swoop of crows.
Surely the conspiracy of parents was right there
in front of that raggedy pair,
striding on such skinny legs
that no distance would ever bridge their hunger.

Still, I rooted for them, all the while knowing
they were truly lost.
The witch was the only helpful guide,
I could breathe again once she entered.
You need something real to fight against and finally
she brought it.
Like little birds captured in their own ribcages,
they sang together then.
Fear is opera and she was a cackling diva in black
delivering on a big scale.
She led them to strike back
and for that she must always die.

By the end I could unclench.
It turns out ok.
The things you know will fail, *will* fail.
There is always a brother or sister to share that trip.
In eating the bread of suffering, you are never alone.
Then, too, there are the eyes
of those who should have loved you,
looking away, turning the heart inside out, a wrung wren,
a stone skipped on an open wound, the splay of want,

Continued

the ache of the kiss fist you just have to face.
But in the end
Trust the Witch,
Trust the Witch.

The Accident Inside

8 a.m. the call
by nine you're there
no one can say
exactly what happened
no one knows
especially not her.

In starchy sheets she lies
so white, so still –
is she breathing?
Of course, of course she's breathing.

From behind a nurse appears
sterile, gray –
she checks the pulse
you check her shoes
the mute soles
crepe, deceptive.

She wrinkles towards you
offers advice
have a seat, dear
then moves from the room
soundless as hallucinations.

The tile floor rises
as if to swallow you.
By the small window
the heat wavers across the pane.
You see it and wonder
what else is silently here –
what else
in this room is not being
said.

She Said:

When you die it's like
the ripeness of watermelon
inside the hard rind
it's too sweet to bear.

There are dark seeds
in every vein
and the clean, scary smell of blood
a forbidden fruit.

When you die it's like
you knew all along
this is the moment you've been
waiting for.

When you die all the black
seeds in your veins
redden and part
a red sea, parted.

The watermelon is ripe
ready to feed you
the rich sugar
of oblivion.

The green just gives way
when you die
but how new, what a surprise to find
yourself fully open.

When you die, finally
something has happened
unlike the nowhere you have been
for months on end.

When you die, thank God
the seeds are dropping
spilling over themselves
onto your own good ground.

Notes From a Hospital Bed

I am stone
skipping across the surface
of water.

Sometimes this is beautiful.
I touch lightly and the eyes
of my grandchildren appear.

Oceans encircled
float by my bedside
then blink away.

Sometimes I touch down
and tubes have grown from my nose.
My heartbeat a harbor light
green in the distance
flashing on/off.

Then the loft
of a wave, a soft dark arm lifting
cradling me
towing me towards
the churning currents.

In the air
across the water
sometimes flung
sometimes freed

skimming sequence
of breath
of touch and go
here and gone
sky and stone

then over again.

Ruth Returns

I am the other daughter.
The one you didn't speak of,
the one you sent away at birth
because you had no name
to give me.

I am the other daughter.
Your eyes look through mine
even after this great weight of years
I know you know me
sight unseen.

I am the other daughter.
The one who drifted through
daydreams, nightmares
you swore one day would fade
as skies clear from rain.

Mother, I ask only this:
Before you go, breathe again
the name you might have given.
Call me daughter,
not other.

Hand Me Downs

That summer, Kory Etta came to live with us in the long wake
of what was only called *the accident*. Mother had already brought
the boxes of hand me downs from the attic. My cousin Kory Etta's
outgrown clothes, my new/old summer wardrobe. She was the
gentlest among us, the one crying and furious when we shot BBs at
birds. That was the summer she ran over the child who chased a ball
into the road. Morbid at twelve, I played that movie in my head all
season long. Frame by frame I filled in the unspoken scenes. I wore
her floral hand me down skirt and sat in our old Pontiac pressing the
air above the accelerator, clenching the steering wheel, driving my
mind to the other side of town. I was her, then him, then her. Then
I would remember that other detail: a white highway patrolman
passing by. The unlikely fortune. I paste it in, a Kodak pop as
miraculous as invention. He sees it all in a flash, no speeding and
no time for swerving. An accident. A sad but unavoidable accident.
This is in his report. His testimony means no trial. I rewind, replay.
The boy sees her blank white scream, she hears a fleeting question
in his dark eyes.

Again, I forget to include the cop passing by. Rewind. Instead, I
see him wink across a courtroom at my cousin. Did I make this up?
What is a little white lie? How little and how white? These reels
were no more real to me then than news on TV, footage of broken
black bodies, brutal baptisms from fire hoses, a German Shepard's
bared teeth. Celluloid collages on a flickering black and white
screen.

In the courtroom, the mother of the boy we never name slumps
inside her skin. My cousin's sedated eyes are averted. All summer
long, she never looks up. Her silent quaking goes unmentioned.
When my mother whispers into the phone, "She's suffered enough,"
I know it is Kory Etta, defender of small birds, she speaks of, not the

mother of five, now four. I play it like a dark game all summer long, box out the size of one small coffin, lie in the dry ditch beside the highway, dig my fingers in the earth. Our house stifled by the heat of what was not said. It was Alabama. It was 1968. It was just an accident.

She Waves Goodbye From the Window

Beneath the suggestion of skin,
an intricate genealogy of bone,
blue bloodlines map
the back of your hand.

For years you were shielded, sheathed
in perpetual and proper white gloves,
until, unveiled, the skin became
a gentle drape of gauze, soft crepe.

Mama, even as you began to fade
into spidery scrawl of your
earlier signature self,
there was a delicate force.

Your last wave lifted and lighted,
brought back a cool touch on summer evenings
when fireflies winked beyond the screens.
Soft, soft as a lullaby, your hands.

Late February

Great Aunt Lela never meant
to freeze that winter.

She had plans
to plant in spring.

The doctor said
she was probably asleep
didn't feel a thing.

"Hypothermia,"
he rasped, "is often gentle
with its victims."

It was late February
when we found her.

Her creased face, an enamel mask,
her delicate wrist crooked
over Irish lace.

Through the window
a watery light washed
over the scene.

She was a pearl
submerged.

Paper Cuts

I cut paper dolls from newsprint
twelve bad memories holding hands
asking for a mother to show
I rip through words
saying pop pop pop
make the weasel pop.

I take the doll-sized dresses
too small to stretch
rip the rows of lace
no one no one no one
to call that gown her own
I yank the stringy hair in rage
all my Barbies bald
I make them ugly
slap their plastic butts say
you be a good girl
good girl, good girl.

I pin my paper dolls to the line
they flip and flop and fly
those hanging sisters call out
bad girl, bad girl, bad girl.

My face stings
my hands twitch
my room's too small
I bang my head on walls so
white they hurt the eyes.

I take my scissors
to my favorite friends
patty cake patty cake
snip snip snip
off goes the hair

off goes the head
the newsprint bleeds
my fingers turn dark
cut those hands that hold
printed confetti
in a nightmare parade
snip and snipe and snarl

these twelve bad dolls cut in pieces
with no heart to hold
and what a mess twelve bad memories
pare away.

Life Magazine: First Blood

She is a ten year old American girl inexplicably adrift
in a napalm village where she sees but cannot comprehend
the stark skin of the burned girl running motionlessly
across the glossy page.
The image sears her eyes.
And though she cannot make her way
through the murky language,
she feels unmistakably *something is wrong*.
The air cries in her ears inconsolably.
Turn the page and an old man emerges from an airplane.
The anger in his face is her father's.
She believes he is trying to tell her something
but she will never know what his scowl means.
Danger pulses around her.
Only one way to slow it, *slow it*.

Her question becomes not how she came to be here,
but how does she get back?
What magic or mark will map the way?

The air flaps against her like a broken wing,
a pulsing uncertainty.
Maybe she is the one who is really not here.
Maybe she is just an image of herself in some magazine.
Maybe she is the story of the girl that she doesn't understand.

She feels herself blur,
senses one way home,
feels her way in the dark for the literal
visceral now
flesh and blood and bone
back to the body,
body is home.

Cutting

Brought me back into my body
the first brilliant red bead, a kiss
like a crimson lip print on my cheek
before mama smudged it away with her thumb.

The soft, pale flesh yielded easily
like a wet May field being plowed.
It made me real again to see
the ordinary elements of life.

How simple: just flesh, just blood after all.
I was careful to seal up the evidence
seeds back in the soil patted over
lipstick rubbed rosy as a blush.

I needed that view of the inside
from time to time, a visual answer
a vermillion encrypted message
from my self to myself.

Cutters

It's a secret society of self.
Hidden hieroglyphics of
a language not yet dead,
not mere scream or whimper,
more like covert communiqués
from the fighting factions within.
A signal that must occur
under cover of one's own flesh.
A skillful coding of the vocabulary of blood,
the sharpened edge of a Rosetta stone poised
for wordless translation.

Scars

Above the eye, an exclamation point
that ended a sentence.
I threw myself over the bars of the crib,
the window sill, an unexpected comma
in that fine phrase.

Embedded in chin skin, just out of sight,
the mark made from a patent leather shoe
heel stabbing in split second slow motion
from the monkey bars above.
My face bloomed vermilion tulips
as the first grade teacher gathered me up,
a delicate bouquet staining her prim
white blouse.

My shins are maps,
crisscrossed routes over and onto
tree stumps, granite, bricks against which
I honed myself during games of chicken,
bike crashes and climbs toward a top branch of sky,
paying little attention to the ground below.

My nose is permanently out of joint,
a winged creature flies across the bridge
an omen from the past that reminds me
not just to watch, but duck, when things fly at me.

On my sole, a jagged river route,
the broken glass under water, an unexpected step,
turned the water miraculously red
that one, biblical in proportion,
closed off feeling forever in that region,
the nerve severed, a wound that changed my walk.

Continued

The delicate wrists frown on themselves slightly,
paper thin incisions,
evidence of the era of embarrassment,
ritual blood letting, sacrifices to edgy angst,
uneasy indents over the hearty ropes of vein.

My body is a book.
I reread the lines to find
the fierce allegory of old adventures.
The more recent passages
are artistically ambiguous.
I touch them as a sighted person
might touch Braille,
hidden in plain view,
a hint at the open ended question.

Backyard

We eat sun-warm figs
just plucked from the tree
our mouths maniacal with pleasure.

Scattered green tongues of grass
flicker toward the outer edges of the garden
graze at the edge of corn rows.

Our hunger leads us forward
towards the lush, gluttonous
arena of summer.

Two

Driving Away From Home

We stop at a fruit stand
where a woman, big and brown,
with melon heavy breasts
scratches her rump and says

Yep. Been a right good spring,
rain and hot sun. Just perfect
for the fruits of the earth.
That's what we got here,
sweet fruit.

She waves the flies away,
scratches.

You thump the cantaloupe, honeydew.
We choose two randomly
and drive away,
the white lines beneath us
fall away like feathers.

When Kill Devil Hills is in sight
where the Wright brothers
dared gravity,
you begin to talk.

I only hover at the outer edges of your words
hearing the low throb of airplanes,
white and thin in the distance,
floating back

I long to push you
out of our small earth bound car
into the careening sky
whispering

fly close.

Wings

We walk the thistle path
on the way to Wright Memorial.
The sun scalds our heads and hands.

From the high sand dune above the sea
it is not hard to imagine anyone daring
to take the sky in his arms.
You tell me about aero-dynamics and seagulls,
I tell you my mother was born out here
and will neither swim nor fly.

At night we put up screens
south of where a private plane
dove into the ocean.
The heron screams before noon,
I spread my arms across the bed
to find you gone.

On the beach
my shadow cuts a path before me.
In the slow summer drone
I begin to run hoping to gather momentum
lift, and finally fly,
my shadow from above
finding and falling over yours below.
I'll practice hovering, swooping, diving.
One day these wings may be strong enough
to dip and gather you up
beautiful sun scaled fish.

Some Nights

In the narrow pocket of my bed
I run my palm across the linen length
to feel your absence
stretching across the dark hours where I lie
wanting to reach you, waking

again the brute flesh of desire
but you are not to be kept
no one to call out to.

In the stillness I imagine your breathing
call your shadow from the wall
move the distance with shapes my fingers make
and promise myself I will put away objects,
museum pieces, shells, words
that no longer belong to you or me.

Then the sound of a motorcycle
tears up the night, light zooms
through my room and takes me

back home, as a young girl
I watched headlights of passing cars dissect
my walls and even then I was restless, waiting.

What You're Waiting For

There is a reassuring immediacy
to waiting in a line
with a cash register at the end.
I'm waiting to pay,
you say securely.
Then the milk and honey will be mine.
The eggs, the bread
the beautiful, glossy still life covers...

Waiting for the doctor or dentist
sooner or later you will be seen,
examined even,
legs or mouth wide open
for the coolly observant eye to appraise
your general well being.

And, of course, the light turns green
eventually. The automatic door opens
before you run into it.
The elevator reaches a certain floor.
Your cheeseburger comes out the little window
neatly bagged and wrapped.

These things happen.
They indicate reason,
a possible conclusion to waiting.

But as day yawns toward close
you come home.
Is there a letter?
Will the phone ring?
Who is driving down this road
so late in the evening?

Some waiting is an uncertain task,
a prolonged twilight.

The carpet is worn from this pacing.
The hard wood floor of the hall only echoes your steps.
The illuminated face of the clock
throws a small, weak light in this hollow room

where you search for the words that will name
what it is you're looking for.

Tracks

Gone.
Even the snow melts away
from the tire tracks,
your last comment.

This morning high in glazed pine branches
a stellar jay tears me from sleep
with an awful caw.

Against the cold early
porcelain of stove and sink,
I drink my coffee black,
lift back the curtain,
squint into the white glare,
watch the thin trickle of an icicle thread down.

Down this window
the rivulets begin to weave
the first vein of spring.

Learning To Say Goodbye

I leave your hands fisted at your sides.
I leave the downward curve of your mouth.
I leave you to whatever is behind the closed lids
you stare into.

I used to wait
thinking the walls would surely shake
the ceiling come crashing down.
I waited for the oven to cease its constant baking,
for the bed to drift out to sea,
some visible clue to what I already knew
something is wrong here.

Nothing happened.
Your hands stilled by your sides
refused to shape the landscape of my skin,
refused any invitation to touch,
unmoving
two hanging birds.

A friend writes to me
everything gathers, gains momentum, builds
toward meaning, though not one we always have words for…
but words have found their way out again
surviving the distracted repetitions,
the absurd collection of nonsense syllables
we have come to speak in.

I leave you having long since been left
untouched, silence compounded by silence.
Words come back as if from a long distance
shaped out of breath

Continued

out of the pulse of memory
that propels me into the day

I have gathered what I need
to leave.

Love Note

In my underwear drawer
under piles of panties and camisoles I never wear
a little love note.

Why save a love note
written by an ex-husband from a time before
he was even husband?

A strange sentimentality
to save these scraps from our scrap heap
of things better off forgotten.

Still, every five years or so,
longer than the marriage lasted,
it surfaces

but does not sing, or even breathe.
It simply marks the place where the past was
written in its own words.

Gallstones

They lodge in the center
every bitter word I've swallowed
the bile of unvoiced anger.
They pile up to sculpt
the wordless weight of interior space.

Their image wavers on the ultrasound screen
washed back in waves from inside out.
I think of walks along wooded paths
where someone has left
a balance of stones, a marker, their passing
made visible to others.

I consider the stone quality of me
reflect on my inner rubble
my rocky center
imagine a still life from still births.

From this jagged pain,
this boiled down scorpion sting, pillar of salt,
this one searing note on the lute of the past
vibrating from the core
sounding an excavation of self
from this dark cavern

there may be something yet to mine.

Still Life With Apples

Something pulls the covers from my sleep.
I wake with a hollow in the bed beside me
and wonder why I am clinging to the edge.
When I drift back away from mute rooms
into dreams where a voice says things like
point du jour, crescendo and *how do ya like them apples?*
I know morning is only minutes away.

I'm in the shower when a woman's voice floats up
from the street outside.
I want to run after her still wet and naked
ask her *would you like to come in? Have coffee?*
I want to ask *How do you like them apples?*
Maybe she will know what that means.

Instead, I pass up coffee along with most of the day.
In the evenings I make sweeping statements to my furniture
or I remind myself there is still a hole in my back
where the bullet was removed.
I tell long tales and wonder afterward
when did the last dog stop barking in the distance?

Even the old piano has no answers. I pound the ivory.
All the keys turn black before me, notes lie flat.
I punch the pedals harder with my feet until
I am racing faster and faster downhill
and crash into blind sheets where I wait
to hear the same voice that trails off every day
with the same question mark.

Bartender At the Veterans' Club

The minute she walks behind the bar,
he clicks his teeth into clichés,
"Just because there's snow on the roof,
don't mean they ain't no fire in the stove."
At 2:00 p.m. it's just the two of them.

His tongue flickers out between his lips,
a grotesque parody of passion meant as
lusty flirtation. She pours him another bourbon,
splashes in some coke. It's her job after all.

She wonders vaguely why he spends everyday,
except Sunday, drinking from 9-5,
as if that's *his* job. And why take Sunday off?
To worship God? See some family?

He was in the second Great War.
He tells her he was a hero in France
"where the women don't wear no underpants"
Eager to reward him, they were on him "like white on rice."
He winks at her as if it's a joke they share.

He totters off just before the other regulars arrive.
Their hands and necks grimy from labor,
their booming voices exploding in the air,
the beer begins an endless flow. Until dinner calls them home.

During the in-between time,
after old Hosea leaves and before the working men barge in,
she tells herself it's temporary, until something better turns up.
Besides it's not so bad she reckons, easy cash, free booze.
Her own clichés are what keep her going.

How She Loves Me

she loves me through the strings of a child's guitar
quietly throbbing the dark after bedtime

I hear her refrain from touching
the moment of mystery, the moment of exactly me

her fingerprint is laughter and fragment of moon
trailing a slow gooseflesh of stars in the skin of the sky

she loves me like sand or snow
drifting away from any ridge of reason

towards the rib of something she will never say
she loves sparingly with words, her truth is in touch

she has given me the deeds to a land of longing
careless as blessing a stranger's sneeze

she shares with me the knowledge of night
in the nod of her head

she loves me as unintentionally as air
my need is the child of her parent

she is the tenor of the choir that lifts me
from my anonymous seat

the guide and witness to my first steps
in a perilous leap of faith

she stamps the letter that opens my heart
the one she carelessly sent

Continued

could I even exist without the colliding
world of her eyes in my orbit?

she is a giant of gentle lapses
lapping a compass of love

she is my direction, neither north, nor south, east, west
all a sameness of her

she breezes through warm tides
with the cooling current of her face

she brings me back to myself
without calling my name

she is the skin under my skin
the image behind the bald eyelid of day

she opens the lid on the collection
of memories I've trapped in a jar

but how to know how to navigate the world
without choosing a name?

her love is the hidden scar of me
the crease of underneath

the unwarranted flesh of desire
the reek of real that nothing can completely cover

truly, if she did not love me, how could I be?

she loves me in the wake of a child's clutch
at the blanket of blue dreaming

moving from the tender wound of bruised birth flesh
into the yellow stare of every day

she loves me like any ordinary thing she sees
passing by on her certain way

Antigone Goes To Town

A sponge of self-
absorbed pain,
she wrings herself out
at parties.

Never completely dry,
she tries to cry out her singular conflict,
but only manages an echo of the universal
why me?

A well-worn drama is
squeezed from morning mishaps;
structured retelling forms
nemesis, tragic flaw…

Well into her third glass
she almost sings.
Her chorus constantly warns:
time, time…

Her climax, self-
banishment to a back bedroom
where no witness
sees her tragic end.

How To Speak Plain English

Out with it.
Don't beat around the bush.
Speak your mind,
mean what you say, say what you mean,
no patois, no pidgin, no slang, no slurring, no exceptions.

Avoid an accent, particularly French,
so affected.
Spit it out
but say it don't spray it.
Come clean.

No spin, no simpering, no stammer, no stutter.
Be direct with your object,
but remember actions speak louder.

Don't get tongue tied.
Use your tongue
like the blunt instrument it is.

Put it in layman's terms.
Be frank.
Get to the point.

Put it in plain English.

No one's listening anyway.

Learning To *Just Be Nice*

I've whittled down the sharp
edges of my tongue
to form a nice squarish block
for the mouth.

I've stretched the shade
over narrowed eyes, wiped the shadow
widened the gaze
to present a more pleasing view.

My head is a slow motion rocker
sedated metronome
agreement, acquiescence, acknowledgement
all implied by a slow nod.

Scrubbed clean of abrasion
I dim the glare, smile, nod
do my part to keep the world
safe from sarcasm.

The Snail Comes To the Flatlands

The snail arrives
makes iridescent paths
disturbs the dust
leaves sticky glitter
signs on walls.

The snail trails
through weeds
up houses
over steps
boundaries
where he leaves his mark.

Crawling through March
he wants to quit
carrying the curled fist
the circular argument on his back.

The snail finishes last in the flatlands
after miles of graffiti
he inches towards the edge
searches for a quarry
to bait fish.

Carson City Drum Circle

The wind whips Carson City
desert air churns up my hair as I walk
past St Charles Hotel and hear the ululating
tongue of drums.

In Comma Courtyard a drum circle draws
together beating in the vivid heat
while I hover unnoticed in the alleyway
a voyeur in the ritual of rhythm.

One speeds up
his hands a brown blur over the taut belly
of his drum.
Another follows
palm, palm, knuckle
palm, palm, knuckle
faster as she sweats and smiles.

I feel the pounding in my center
echoing inside out
waves of salt and fire of thunder
streaming stream of human touch
these hands at the heart
of all the pulsing world.

Blue Trajectory: A Photograph Of
a Cliff Diver Off the Coast Of Menorca

for Ignacio

Two worlds divided/united by your body.
You are suspended between blue above and blue below.
One fluid movement stilled and held.

We hold to what we want most.
So what did she think, the one whose eye held you,
then gave you those miraculous wings?

There are no nets for this bold flight.
No feathers, wax, nor any chase,
pura vida just soaring breath and breathless pause

between the seamless sky and sea below.
Your arms as strong and fragile as a sudden gust of wind
against the unseen cliff behind you.

Translation

Which language can I use to speak to you?
Most are closed to me, the foreign syntax of worlds not my own,
the signs translate differently, a cultural rift.

When you lift my hair off my neck,
I want you to press your lips just there, but you give a quick fan
and drop the locks back into place, damp, clinging tendrils.

For language we have touch or laugh
until our eyes slide out to sea, awash in what we can not say.
The horizon widens its interminable blue ache.

A Bar In Bavaria

My English speaking host has wandered off to chat up a girl who
looks like a label peeled from a bottle of beer. I'm surrounded
by rapid fire German that flies over my head, unknowable as a
dialect of zippers. When my face starts to freeze, I reach for a mug,
something wordless and real for my hands and my lips. I try to
attune myself to the tone of this tribe, pay close attention to cues.
When smiles start to fade, I set my lips straight in a line, furrow
my brow. When everyone escalates, syllables clashing like cymbals
rising towards some mad crescendo, I lean in, eyebrows lifting. And
then, the epiphanous moment when laughter erupts, I grin, happy
as the village idiot: a sound I understand, one knowable moment
in this guttural collective. After an hour I'm maudlin with beer, so
alone in this genial group of Germans. My face is tired of trying. I
want to go home. I cover my yawning mouth with my hand hiding
this exile from speech.

Au Pair

I mind their children, the sweet but slow one, the constantly
drooling Eglantine,
and the evil one, Jean Olivier.

J.O. introduces himself by smacking me in the shin with a tin truck.
His mother, Monique, says vaguely as if words exhaust her, "J.O.,
arrête."

Both children shriek at the sight of bath water, but Monique has
firmly closed the door behind her, on her way to the evening's
aperitifs.

One day I offer to help the other hired hand. Madame-a-la-cuisine
half sniffs, half snorts at my mangled version of "may I help you
wash the vegetables?" She breaks eggs in a bowl, then beats them
furiously until I leave.

That same day I have a head throbbing epiphany: J.O. is the only
child I've ever hated. His sing song taunt "Cassez les bras, cassez
les jambs" echoes through the long afternoon. Monique doesn't
comment on his pleasantries, merely rolls her world-weary eyes.

When I retire to the sanctuary of my solitary room, I smoke a
Gaulois too harsh to inhale, sip a punishing eau de vie, close my
eyes, and imagine the France of my dreams.

The August Air Of DC

It's heavy. Oppressive as the sweaty hug of your least favorite uncle. Worse. A wet, sloppy kiss from him. Your clothes absorb the humidity from the air around you, start to stick to your skin, hang, pull you down to any bench or chair you happen by. Sitting doesn't help. The air masses its watery weight around you. Nothing is fun any more. The animals at the zoo are listless and you pretend to shoot them, index finger and thumb pointing the blame, bang, bang as if they're responsible for the muggy heat. You stay inside the panda house for as long as you can, there's some shade at least, but so many other sweaty bodies are circling that the polite orbit is soon lost and their salty skin is touching your own. I will scream, you think. If one more person touches me I will jump right into the Panda pen, but then looking at their fur makes you suddenly itchy. Even the sharp sirens constantly slicing the haze get muffled, edge blunted by the eroding air. A gray pall shrouds the distance. This town has a killing air.

Seagulls In Vancouver

Such posers. Outside my hotel room one perches atop St Mary's hospital, above the illumined white cross. Pretensions of seagull sainthood, regal half turns of the head. I try to wait him out, stay on the balcony until he finally flies off, but it gets too wet and cold. He wins. I go in and flip on the TV. The Pope is dying today. It's on every channel. I pull the curtain back and the seagull is still posed, a gargoyle on the spire of St Mary's. I assume it's the same seagull, how to know? They come dressed alike and can take each other's place so quickly, a flap, a swoop that sudden gathering into stillness. He presides over this spot in the city, preposterously regal from his point on the tower, a wing of white smoke webbed in gray. How so still? Why not swoop down for some street level crumb? He doesn't seem natural. Maybe he knows something is up. Maybe a benediction rises from the halls and elevators, the sick beds and offices of St Mary's, some collective mourning spirit funnels up, all the way to the spire that holds the bird in thrall, a figure so transient and unmoving, a gesture to the sky.

The Mannequins Of Vancouver

First they came across the Granville Bridge, rolled on a trolley by what appeared to be graduate students in baseball caps. Made in their image, Mannequins: male and female they were. And very white. And unclothed. Rolled out in a column like marvelous Greek forms. They had heads but no eyes, no hair. They were there to be seen, not to see. Later that same day their white figures appeared on a street corner announcing an event, a show, some gathering or happening. Still unclothed, pasted with flyers, standing on more flyers, announcing something not to be missed. The other ones, behind the plate glass shop windows, were so well dressed I wanted to weep. Even the homeless chic attire was finely presented, no match for the real thing. I felt embarrassed, poorly clad. Then came the headless ones. This is an interesting human form, mannequins with no heads but beautiful, perfect, upright breasts. At least they had what mattered chilling inside those picture windows. The males were all the same, though, headless or not. I felt in commune with a strange population. The traveling nude white tribe making art announcements, the headless, the full-headed but hairless, the ones with eyes, the ones with nipples, the ones with much too little or nothing at all. The last one waved me goodbye from a shop in the airport. She had a head, which I was very thankful for, and painted eyes that appeared to look, but best of all, her hair was multicolored and spiked. She was my favorite. I name her Zora. I have my picture taken with her because I feel a sudden kinship. I think she will miss me. For days I have been awash in a sea of people and distant mannequins, but just before I leave the city to return to my little life in the mountains, I make a connection. It's a love story of sorts. The one you meet before flying away, the one who could really love you, the one you know you love. Zora. I have her picture. I'll never forget her.

county fair girl

tilt
                  whirl
                             swirl of cotton
candy
 pink

Elevator

A medieval torture, perfected. Waiting to climb into these tiny
cubicles of movement, waiting, waiting, endlessly waiting, thinking:
are these just painted images? Are these doors even real? Why do
they never open? And then they do. Hellishly. They open onto
567 smashed together humans in a little reeking windowless box, a
moving coffin. Useless. You'll have to wait some more. You think *I
could use the stairs* and then remember your destination on the 777th
floor. *Fuck*, you can't help but say. Your hands are shaking, you want
water, you need to get on the damn elevator. You try to will your
weight into a blue bubble that might rise above this, all your hot
air lifting you off to where you wish to land. It doesn't work. Your
head's on too loose and your mind wanders. The waiting has now
formed a congregation who begin to sing along to muzak tunes from
prehistory, praying to the numbers, counting down, 67, 66, 65, and
then the chanting starts. People are praising the floor numbers,
a spontaneous hallelujah erupts. A voice in the wilderness cries
out "almost there" but it has been 40 years already and we're still
stranded on this floor. People start to suggest procuring a new god.
One that works. Maybe something in gold.

Altars

City Lights, San Francisco

Angel haired hipsters still hover. I drift upstairs, drawn to the open
window. Across the alleyway a woman has hung clothes out her
window: skimpy panties, swathes of silk, robes doing the opposite
of drying in this mist-heavy air. I pull myself back in the room and
breathe the incense of old books, yellowed page embrace, loving
mother tongue speaking in ancient voices. I open my eyes to see
long lost professors howling words to the wind, sisters whisper
secrets from the corners, so many of the glorious dead speaking
in tongues that I feel on the verge of being able to interpret. I've
entered the holy upper room, ineffable space, shrine filled with the
spirits of those bards iconicly hung on the walls. Here I could kneel,
a small space open to the universe.

Three

Panning Gold

The bald eye of sun glares into dappled pine
for the brief flicker of chickadee, listening
mules ears.

In the yellow haze of midday heat
a snicker of stream bares its sandy teeth, glinting
fools gold.

Mountain buttercups chin up to yellow grasses
insect shells empty below pollen motes, floating
straw bridge.

Shapechanging

The wind rattles against the window.
You stand in the center of the room
but also appear cast across the wall.
The streetlight has recreated this place
in geometric shapes from the fire escape outside.

You move from frame to frame.
I watch your silhouette knowing
you are not easy to see,
shapechanger, coyote.
The play of shadows, the tilt of your head,
or your slink towards me,
may reveal or conceal you.

Outstretched, our fingers appear to connect.
We begin a sleight of hand on the bedroom wall.
When we let our hand shadow birds fly loose
they escape around a corner
then dive in again from the ceiling.
I watch your hands make wings.
In flight they call me to follow
a new trajectory of touch.

Intrusions

You come unasked for
a barnacle on my private shell
the thing in a basket a stranger leaves
who rings the bell then runs.

I think of your unexpected arrival
in a brief spasm of union
the salt that brought you here
not enough to carry you
to a place you could call home.

Your frail question is answered.
I pluck you from me
strange anemone
set you awash
in the awful sea I loose.

Trying On Mother's Shoes

For the third time, still they do not fit
stretched so large in places I just slip
and tell you that I love you
knowing what need I betray.
You say nothing, just hum the rhyme
your father sang you to sleep by.

When we pass the Kiddie Korner
with all the white boots dangling
small enough for dolls the blankets, baskets
you stare too long and I notice
though I only look ahead.

For the third time I have let slip from me
the small curled fist, the milky eyes,
broken off some bud of continuity.

You do not speak, and the air
between us wells with absence.
Mother's shoes, the ones she gave me
because my feet had spread
like hers, she said
hang, empty pockets on the back
of my closet door.
I cannot walk in them,
cannot, yet, give them up.

Out the Window

Snow covers all, icicles lunge from eaves,
sentries of pine, bristle against the stilled sky.

A street paved white with snow and ice
leads to a shrouded distance.

Naked aspens rake furrows in the mist,
scratch toward light, claw at the oppressive white.

In Winter

There is a secret being told to the earth.
Snow drifts with quiet force,
sculpting another world out of this one.

A whisper moves across the landscape,
coaxes the earth to breathe in a new way.

I have the urge to reach out a gloveless hand,
to lift the snow without fear of freezing or burning,
to hold the intimacies gathering here and find the half-seen worlds
shaped by silence.

I want to lie down, be covered by this strange linen,
allow an arrangement in the angles of my body
so my edges soften and round until
even the shadow I cast becomes subtle and new.

The Third Month

Morning becomes more
outside branches begin
to take on their true forms
berries, blueblack, glazed
pull from the limbs.

Last night I strained to hear
past the rain, for a car
a click of heels, a voice
a knock at my own door.
I turn under the weight of blankets
wishing for spring.
I curl and bunch as though I, too, might
swell and fall.

These nights of waiting have been mapped
by the moon-cast webs on my wall.
Rain has become an unsteady pulse
quickening inside, outside.
I stare at the perfectly round berries
in the early frost light and remember
a child who looked up
and said *bloodberry*
blood
berry
to no one in particular.

Forgotten Dream Sequence

1
I had forgotten desire
until it came back in a dream
lifted me out of my body
scraped my bones until
their hollow whistle
was the music of longing.

2
The dream seeps away.
I lie still and taut
try to recover all of it
but too much is lost on waking.
Only one image hovers:
I slip out of myself
I pull off layers
peel the outer husks
until I become true as air.

3
I forget that I can't fly
so I fly
through air, through water
through time, the cold dark of space
perforated with lights and voices.
One says *I was Taymoor.*
For days after I wonder
whose voice was that?
Should I know?

4
Try to forget the sting of a slap:
you'll hear its red echo all night long.
Try to forget the kiss of betrayal:
you'll close your eyes and night will stitch them up.
Try to forget the teeth in the mute trap:
you'll walk down halls doomed to open door after door
into empty rooms whose dark throats swallow you whole.

5
In my dream I wake up.
I rise like steam over a coffee cup.
I am relieved it is so easy to move.
I drift down the stairs and spread through the room.
I try to remember how it was before.
Why did I ever struggle?
Movement is like breathing now,
not the hard pull of anchor out of elements.
Then, just the memory of that pull becomes static,
a gray tone vibrating and dispersing.
I know I can't stay.
Already the weights of limbs reach for me.

6
I look down at myself sleeping.
I feel tender, as a mother might.
I feel a distant sympathy
rumpled sheets, frowning sleep
head heavy on the pillow
fingers curled like empty cups.
There is something I want to say
to the sleeper,
there is something gentle and healing
I am trying to remember.

Remembering Tinky's

"Sometimes you get shown the light in the strangest of places if you look at it right." Robert Hunter

We were always drunk when we went to Tinky's, had to be just to go there. Sprouted between two fields, that desperate little shack with two gas pumps out front was a thumbnail of redneck honky tonks. Ro played fiddle some weekends there in a drop-in bluegrass band. Confederate flags littered the cement walls like swatted bugs. Tinky, the 300 pound bartender, served up the Buds with a gap toothed grin. The tin roof played its own timpani when the rain came, then the band could play along or just plain quit, there was no way of getting over it. One bathroom, special for the ladies, was added like a second thought in a lean to on the side of the building. One steamy drunk night I'm waiting with the other ladies for that blessed single toilet when a big old woman grabs my hand and starts to dance with me. "I don't know how to..." I stammer in speech and step. She shouts in my face like I'm standing in North Dakota, "Girl, everyone needs to know how to two step." She appoints herself my dance instructor then and there in our elevator-sized ballroom, other ladies hooting and howling. I step on everyone's toes including my own. No one ever had to pee as much as I did right then. Finally, finally her turn at the toilet comes, then mine. I make my escape on Ro's next break. As I'm heading out the door the old woman hollers, "Girl, you just need to learn to quit thinking about *yourself* and dance." Speeding down Camden highway in the backseat, I perfect a cackling imitation of her voice. Our laughter whips out the car windows, lashes out into the night splicing the sweet smell of corn. It's taken me years, centuries of standing still to realize she was right all along. That crazy old woman got it right.

In Spring

After the rain, the drumbeat
awakens the blood, the heart blooms,
circles from itself toward the sun.

We breathe back into our bodies
the wood rose air of ancient joys
cup the dragonfly sky in our palms.

We emerge from ourselves like serpents
leave the old scales and skin, the sediment
the layers of separation, all behind us.

We swallow the sea and the salt
allow this birth once again, this beginning
green eye that opens each year anew.

Message To Myself In May

Part the flesh of the old skin you're in.
Push away from the sediment of self.
Rub the rock of rebirth, open your back on the bark.

Shed the ungainly cells, the habit of sameness.
Suspend separation, breathe seamlessly into begin.
Speak up the lightening language of sky.

Open the wings of watery blue on dry land and above.
Hatch from the horizon of flesh-bruising birth.
Rise from dim shallows into the iridescence of pulse.

Call yourself into the summer.
Light out for the light with your heart in your mouth.
Emerge softly new in the green fields of yes.

Traveling

Having finally exhausted
the battered vehicle of cynicism,
both shield and weapon,

I stopped
where you were waiting
within and without.

Your finger traces
and erases lines in my face
from then to then to now.

It surprises me
how these old wounds
could map the route to you.

Chrysanthemums and the Communist Manifesto

for Deirdre

What I have to offer you
is a mixed bag of goods:
a yellow chrysanthemum
sunny bright bloom with its whiff of death,
a book whose illicit pages held
a rusty key I needed once

yellowed pages brittle with age
flowers dried between words
maps and moments combined
to create the place that was
the place becoming, the place at a distance
where points converge.

My life converges with yours
and I hand you what I have:
a flower that beams with sun may stink.
The world may stink and no easy way to fix it
but words ripen in the mind.
Some moments make the heart bloom
their fruit and flower
may be just enough
to live by.

The Wall

After passing through so many monuments to wars, we come to the
Vietnam wall. As we walk, the dark stone slowly rises above us with
its tableau of names and people rubbing those names onto pages
they will bear home, the ones mourning, laying wreaths, hugging
themselves together, those in wheelchairs, the living bearing witness
to the dead. The seemingly endless scroll of dead takes on its own
epic hellishness, death unmanned so many and so many returned
incomplete, disarmed, legless, memory seared into the flesh. My son
walks beside me. By the time we reach the center, neither of us is
ashamed to cry openly. I was his age as we raged with Vietnam, the
older boys in town waited for their numbers to come up. My son
watches images of Iraq on TV and asks again where his uncle is. I
say "Tikrit" which means: unknown to us. It means we're afraid and
we speak little of it. The wall in its implacable dark granite offers
no consolation. The list of the dead is a stone weight we must carry
until the bodies of our boys are no longer flown home in black bags.

Howling Rose

for Allison

Moon slivered girl, beautiful and various as blue,
your wrists lashed by your own wordless siren song
of anguished oceans and angry inner gods who grew
weary of beating against the rib of all that felt so wrong.
You wove those wounds into words that led you
to find your voice anew, gave you breath enough to sail,
named your power to create, a source to see you through.
Your power to destroy, its twin, still lurks beyond the pale.
Both brought you to this shore you call your home,
this place where sun and ice combine in your prism eyes
bright from tears and laughter, that divide you roam
never entirely free of fears, but always free of lies.
Your howling rose to fashion words from death by night
into life as fierce, fragile and full of promise as morning light.

My Girl

I think of her, beautiful as the son who managed to get born.
Sunny girl dimpled with baby fat, fly away hair, dandelion.

I imagine her in an Easter dresses, in cut off jeans,
in the back yard baking mud pies, perhaps tasting a few.

Then I see in her a girl that was me; the before time, a child
too young to throw a child away, ragged doll in hand.

But she wouldn't be that age now. This may be the season
when she would hate her mother, do anything to not be like her.

That won't happen. Add it to the other things that also won't:
Her gurgling laugh, a wedding dress, another child who might have
been.

The Trampoline

My son has found another key to the sky.
He lofts himself so high he pulls the air from me.
Watching him, waiting until I can breathe a full breath,
I see him framed in blue. I see him turn

and my stomach turns. I rest my palm over my middle,
the way I did when I first felt him move, roll and kick.
Was the joy and the panic in equal measures then?
Was he bound to strive against any and all bounds?

He wants me to see it all, calls *Watch this!* every time I turn away,
so I stay and cheer a little insincerely: *Beautiful back flip!*
Yes, that probably was six feet of air!
But I think *too much, too high.*

Much too high, dear boy, though I know you'll continue to fly,
the space of sky between you and me will grow larger than both of
us.
For now we measure it in a span of arms, wings, spanning a time
when your life rounds off mine, a high turn against the blue bounds.

Palms

The trees make their mark on the sky,
your name is on my breath.
I want to kneel, feel my knees press
into the earth, very close the roots of trees
are like ancient, strong fingers.

A bird lifts into the evening sky
another flies below,
then, as if moved by the same wing
they glide to rest on the same branch.

The whorls and lines across old trees
make rare palms against the sky
signal a secret language
a silence older than love.

Following the flight of birds
we see the sky more clearly:
how horizon may join two worlds
the way a bird joins the sky
the way trees join the earth
the way we join each other.

Your fingers are brown and strong
like earth, like trees
when you pull me to you
I move rising and rooted,
the strength of earth below
above, the free stretch of sky.

The Ordinary Day Begins

At my desk
the screen blinks on.
Numbers begin their race
but inside me, the throb
of your last morning thrusts
continue, echo
you in me.

The quiet seep of love spreads.
I smile in secret,
the computer hums.
I, too, am humming, low
waves receding
washes of warm light.

Figures flit and flash
numbers, columns, rows
I stare and suck my lower lip
that tastes of you.
Your last kiss lingers
long after the ordinary day begins.

A Lullaby

for Dylan

Sleep little pickle
in your warm bed
you've had your last tickle
and pat on the head.

Sleep little french fry
under warm cover
this is your lullaby
you're loved like none other.

About the Author

June Sylvester Saraceno is originally from Elizabeth City, North Carolina. She received a BA from East Carolina University and an MFA in creative writing from Bowling Green State University in Ohio. Her work has appeared in various journals including *California Quarterly, Ginosko, The Pedestal, Poetry Motel, The Rebel, Silk Road, Smartish Pace, Sunspinner, Tar River Poetry* and *The Village Rambler*; as well as two anthologies: *Intimate Kisses: the poetry of sexual pleasure* and *Passionate Hearts: the poetry of sexual love,* now in a second printing. Her chapbook *Mean Girl Trips* was published fall 2006 by Pudding House Press. She is currently English Program Chair at Sierra Nevada College, Lake Tahoe and founding editor of the *Sierra Nevada College Review*.

She lives with her husband, Anthony Saraceno, and son, Dylan Victor, in Truckee, California.

Photo by Anthony Saraceno, 2005.

Printed in the United States
82208LV00001B/37-135

9 781891 386879